Silver Burdett Picture Histories

The American West

Jean-Louis Rieupeyrout
Illustrated by José Maria Miralles

Translated by Linguassist
from La Vie privée des Hommes: Au temps de la conquête de l'Ouest
first published in France in 1979 by
Librairie Hachette, Paris

© Librairie Hachette, 1979. Adapted and published in the
United States by Silver Burdett Company, Morristown, N.J. 1982 Printing.

ISBN-0-382-06586-7
Library of Congress Catalog Card No. 80-54637

7084

Contents

"When I can hear my neighbor's gunfire . . ."

Total population of the United States	
1870	38.6 million
1900	76 million

Indian population of the United States	
1492	approximately 1,000,000
1900	approximately 250,000
1979	approximately 1,650,000

When and where did the westward migration begin? No one is able to say for sure. We know only that beginning in the 17th century, some English settlers who had been living in the Atlantic coastal towns of New England moved inland. They were said to have gone "to the other side of the hedge," that is, beyond the wooden stockades that protected these settlements from Indian attacks. On Sundays, pastors used to preach from their pulpits against these runaways from civilization who now lived "out there where the bronzed serpents prowl"—referring to the Indians. Where had they gone? Toward the source of the rivers descending from the Appalachians, the low mountains to the west. Why had they gone? In order to be free. Because they had quickly grown tired of the laws imposed by the governor in the name of the king of England. Because they had had enough of the harsh religious rule of the pastors, enemies of the smallest pleasures. These men and women chose an unconfined life in the heart of the wilderness.

A NEW LIFE

Thus began the migration toward the West—the first West—toward the unknown land. These pioneers, with their axes, made clearings in the deep forests. They cut the trees into logs to build their cabins. The surroundings were cleared and the soil was tilled to turn the earth into arable land bearing harvests of corn and wheat. To this they added the game from their hunting trips, poultry (hens, chickens, and turkeys) from their modest farmyards, milk from one or two cows, and meat from their pigs. Women spun wool from their sheep into yarn on spinning wheels. All the family's needs were filled by the constant labor of the family members—food, clothing, kitchen utensils (except for the cast-iron pot), furniture, farming tools, etc. It was as if life was starting all over, and it was, beginning only with the materials that nature provided.

These pioneers belonged to the race described by the famous writer James Fenimore Cooper, author of *The Last of the Mohicans*. His book was one of the tales of adventure inspired by this first period of westward migration. Among its heroes, the pioneer Natty Bumpo tells of the continuous search for a better land: "When I can hear my neighbor's gunfire, it's time for me to move on." And it was true—the pioneers could not stand still, always haunted by the call of the unclaimed West.

TOWARD THE MISSISSIPPI

In the latter part of the 18th century, increasing numbers of these hunter-farmers crossed the Appalachian Mountains and descended the western slopes. They beheld there a land of beautiful grasslands, peaceful streams, and rich forests with clearings where they built hamlets, villages, and the beginnings of towns. For years, the flow of pioneers continued to this region—the second West—which ended only at the Mississippi River. They formed a society that was new in its way of life, its customs, and its outlook; one based on a love of adventure, on courage and endurance. Such were the deerskin-clad fellow countrymen of Davy Crockett, the Tennessee frontiersman, storyteller, and politician who was a living legend in his time. These pioneers did not know that they were building a truly American civilization, different in many ways from the one they had abandoned in the East. They lived simply, day by day, without worrying about playing hero.

Unfortunately, the unrelenting advance of these determined settlers chased the Indians from their ancestral domains. This was the sad opposite side of the coin. By the time the pioneers reached the Mississippi around 1820, the Indians had already suffered a great deal. Worn out and defeated by bloody wars, they were fleeing to the lands on the far side of the river. Only pain and sorrow awaited those who resisted and encountered the treachery of

Twenty years of growth in the West

States	1870	1900
Arizona	9,658	122,391
California	560,247	1,485,053
Montana	20,795	243,329
New Mexico	91,874	195,310
Oregon	90,923	413,356
Texas	819,579	3,048,710
Utah	86,786	276,749
Washington	23,955	518,103
Wyoming	9,118	92,531

U.S.I.S.

Number of immigrants entering the U.S.

1830	23,322
1850	369,980
1870	387,203
1900	448,572
1914	1,218,480

politicians and the harshness of soldiers. Some of these Indian nations had achieved a high degree of social order and comfort in their way of life. Moreover, they had often helped the whites overcome their difficulties in these frontier areas. The whites, in return, forgot the services rendered by the Indians and often treated them as wild animals who had to be exterminated before settlers could safely occupy their lands. This unfortunate situation continued until the end of the saga of the West.

THE "GREAT AMERICAN DESERT"

Would this saga end on the banks of the great Mississippi River? Explorers and geographers who had ventured to the great plains beyond the river thought so around 1840. They were firmly convinced that only Indians and buffalo could live in that immense region of plains abutting the Rocky Mountains—convinced to such an extent that they named it the Great American Desert. However, as early as 1822, the first wagon trains loaded with goods destined for Santa Fe, in what would later be New Mexico, proved that men and animals could survive there. Later, emigrants heading for the Oregon territory and the Pacific coast crossed this "desert" and the mountainous barriers in their "prairie schooners," the canvas-covered Conestoga wagons. In 1847, the Mormons daringly succeeded in settling near the Great Salt Lake in Utah. There they built their capital, Salt Lake City, and spread their culture. Hence, the Great American Desert did not totally deserve its name. It could be conquered despite the dangers present in some regions, and in spite of the severe climate. Subsequent wagon trains took this into account during the great migrations of the 1850s and 1860s.

THE FLOW OF PIONEERS

Following the stagecoaches and the fast riders of the Pony Express, the railroad victoriously linked the East to the West, from the Atlantic coast to the Pacific coast, in 1869. The railroad was crucial to the penetration and development of large areas of wilderness, where farmers planted their crops, and where cowboys rode herd over cattle. The railroad and the telegraph, which was completed in 1861, gave confidence to those who wished to acquire new land. Millions arrived and settled in the most fertile areas, establishing their farms and their villages, which were soon to become cities. The gold and silver rushes had already pushed the fortune seekers toward the mountain gorges. (These "treasure hunts" did not cease until the end of the century, despite the disappointment of most of the participants.)

In half a century—that is, in less than a person's lifetime—the West was the stage of a gigantic adventure. The courageous people who moved westward were seeking a new life, happier if possible than the one they had given up in the East or in their homeland across the sea. However, the life they sought was never just lying there waiting for them. It had to be conquered; this is why books talk about the "taming" of the West. These people had to struggle in order to survive and to build productive futures. They paved the way for all the later crowds attracted by the seductive mirage of the western lands. And so the West was populated. A new America was born, bearing little resemblance to the old one in the East. The people of this new land thought and lived differently from those they had left behind.

This book retraces the major events of this great saga of westward migration. It deals with an era that starts with the arrival of the first Europeans—the Spaniards—in 1540, and ends around 1900. This adventure story, spanning more than three centuries, is a thrilling tale of courage and success, of pain and defeat, of the growth of a nation and a people. It has been reconstructed from the testimony left by each period—paintings, lithographs, archive photographs, and films, selected for their faithfulness to the past, as well as written records of various kinds. These documents were used as points of reference in recreating the reality of yesteryear.

Now it is time to invite you to follow the advice of Horace Greeley, the head of an important New York newspaper, who in 1859 said to young Americans, "Go West, young man, and grow up with the country!"

IDAHO HISTORICAL SOCIETY

Transportation picks up speed

1850	Sailing ships take 90 days to travel from New York to San Francisco via Cape Horn.
1850	Mail travels faster between the same ports. Steamers transport it from New York to Panama, then from Panama to San Francisco (the canal did not yet exist).
1858	The Butterfield stagecoach links Tipton (near St. Louis, Missouri) to San Francisco (California) in 23 days and 23 hours (p. 38).
1860–1861	The Pony Express carries the mail from St. Joseph (Missouri) to San Francisco (California) in 10 days (p. 40).
1879	It takes no more than 7½ days to go by train from New York to San Francisco! (p. 42).

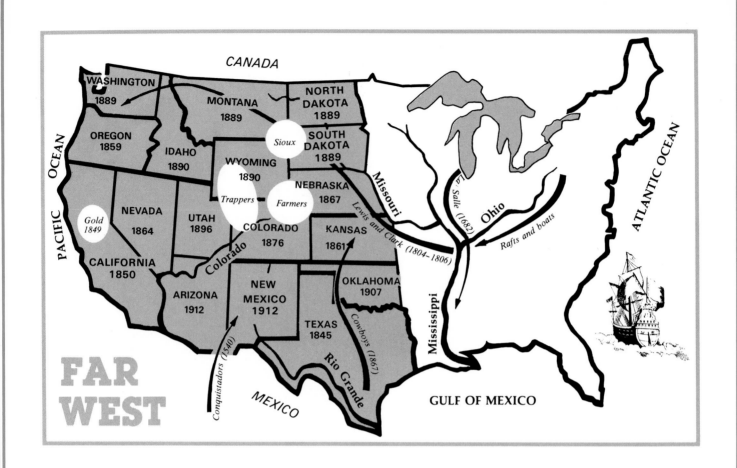

CANADA

WASHINGTON 1889

MONTANA 1889

NORTH DAKOTA 1889

OREGON 1859

IDAHO 1890

SOUTH DAKOTA 1889

Sioux

WYOMING 1890

NEBRASKA 1867

NEVADA 1864

UTAH 1896

Trappers

Farmers

COLORADO 1876

KANSAS 1861

Gold 1849

CALIFORNIA 1850

Colorado

ARIZONA 1912

NEW MEXICO 1912

OKLAHOMA 1907

TEXAS 1845

Missouri

La Salle (1682)

Ohio

Lewis and Clark (1804–1806)

Rafts and boats

Mississippi

ATLANTIC OCEAN

Cowboys (1867)

Rio Grande

Conquistadors (1540)

MEXICO

GULF OF MEXICO

PACIFIC OCEAN

FAR WEST

The 17 States of the American West

State	Capital	Statehood	Area in km²	Motto
Arizona	Phoenix	February 14, 1912	29,510	God enriches
California	Sacramento	September 9, 1850	420,000	I have found it
Colorado	Denver	August 1, 1876	269,200	Nothing without Providence
North Dakota	Bismarck	November 2, 1889	183,500	Liberty and union, now and forever: one and inseparable
South Dakota	Pierre	November 2, 1889	199,550	Under God the people rule
Idaho	Boise	July 3, 1890	217,300	May you last forever
Kansas	Topeka	January 29, 1861	213,063	To the stars through difficulties
Montana	Helena	November 8, 1889	380,800	Gold and silver
Nebraska	Lincoln	March 1, 1867	200,000	Equality before the law
Nevada	Carson City	October 31, 1864	286,700	All for our country
New Mexico	Santa Fe	January 6, 1912	314,000	It grows as it goes
Oklahoma	Oklahoma City	November 16, 1907	181,440	Labor conquers all things
Oregon	Salem	February 14, 1859	250,400	The Union
Texas	Austin	December 29, 1845	688,600	Friendship
Utah	Salt Lake	January 4, 1896	220,100	Industry
Washington	Olympia	November 11, 1889	176,000	By and by
Wyoming	Cheyenne	July 10, 1890	251,228	Equal rights

Conquistadors and Indians

The collision of two worlds. In 1540 an expedition of Spanish conquistadors left Mexico and arrived in the valley of the Rio Grande. This region, totally unknown to the Europeans, would later be called New Mexico. These Spanish conquerors were the first Europeans to penetrate the vast lands of North America. They thought they would discover gold and savages to whom they would bring civilization and Christianity. Instead, they met a perfectly organized Indian society. Well-built villages sometimes housed several hundred people. For this reason, these Indians were called Pueblos, which means "villages" in Spanish. Their descendants living in New Mexico are still called by this old Spanish name.

Established farmers, the Pueblos lived in towns in the Rio Grande Valley. Their ancestors settled there several centuries prior to Christopher Columbus's discovery of the New World. In the fields close to the villages, they cultivated corn (their basic cereal), gourds, beans, tobacco, and cotton, which they used to weave blankets and clothes. They lived in two- or three-story houses, each floor being recessed to form a terrace. Their building materials were either dry stone or adobe, a mixture of earth and straw, which had been dried and hardened in the sun.

The Spanish introduced horses, sheep, and cattle, as well as the wheel, the plow, iron tools and weapons, the bread oven, and even a new god. This was the beginning of the colonization of the Indians. The Pueblos seemed to tolerate their new situation fairly well.

10

The conquistadors arrive in Taos, one of the large Pueblo villages, which still exists.

The men cultivated the cornfields and the women ground the kernels of corn on flat stones with a roller. From one grinding stone to another, they obtained a finer and finer flour, used to make bread dough.

Pottery, one of the Pueblos' most ancient arts, was made by the women. Without a potter's wheel, they made (and still make) magnificent, finely decorated vessels. Today, the same as in the past, each village has its own recognizable style.

From the 12th century on, the Pueblos were the only Native American builders of multiple-story dwellings. The rapid growth of the population of some of their villages forced them to build additional rooms on top of existing ones.

The Spanish monks designed the churches and other buildings of all the missions in New Mexico. The Indians built them under the supervision of the monks. They also cultivated the surrounding fields according to European farming methods, thus providing food for their conquerors. The Pueblos lost their freedom and were converted to Christianity, but they did not forget their ancient gods.

The French settle St. Louis

"**My name is Pierre Lacléde.** My parents were French settlers from Louisiana, the beautiful territory in America that was offered to King Louis XIV by M. Cavelier de La Salle. This is where, in 1764, on the banks of the Mississippi, together with thirty other pioneers, I founded a village which we named St. Louis in honor of King Louis IX. To tell you the truth, the place was first called 'Shortbread,' since in the difficult beginnings we often went hungry. The lack of oxen and plows prevented us from cultivating the land around us. Our main activity was fur trade with the Indians. They were our suppliers. In return, we gave them iron tools, kettles, blankets, and beads. This explains why St. Louis was a town of merchants from its very beginning.

"In 1770, it numbered a hundred wooden houses and about fifteen stone houses, which we were very proud of. Corn and wheat were cultivated nearby. We raised cattle and horses. The population now included craftsmen, blacksmiths, and various tradesmen besides some rich fur merchants who became the notables of the town. In 1803, we changed owners, because Napoleon sold Louisiana to the United States. This did not change our way of life, since we had been settled for a very long time by then. We pursued our activities together with the settlers coming from the American East. They were so numerous that we soon became a minority. Our good old Louisiana grew and expanded before our very eyes. St. Louis became an important and busy city, close to the entrance to the Missouri River, the future route to the enormous interior of the great West."

Pierre Lacléde and his French companions founded St. Louis. This picture shows trees being cut down to build fences and houses. Even as the settlers work, their guns seem to be kept close at hand.

12

The construction of a fort or of the first houses of a village required a great deal of work on the part of the pioneers. From the trunks of felled trees they carefully shaped the logs necessary to build walls.

New families soon joined the population of these first towns in Louisiana. Coming from Canada or from the French port of New Orleans, these families arrived in Indian canoes. Here we see a warm welcome being given to new arrivals.

Houses multiplied little by little, thanks to cooperative effort. The completion of a house was a small event enthusiastically celebrated by all. The French founded several villages in the Mississippi Valley during the 17th century.

Fur trade was the main activity of the people in St. Louis. In exchange for their bundles of furs, the Indians, who were very friendly in this area, received French goods. Long bargaining was often necessary.

The long journey of two captains

An incredible expedition. In 1804, the American captains Lewis and Clark left St. Louis, traveled up the Missouri River, crossed the Rocky Mountains of the Northwest, and reached the Pacific Ocean. Forty men took part in this first transcontinental expedition. Their voyage began on an 18-meter-long keelboat, propelled by a square sail set to catch the wind or by the passengers using long poles in shallow water. Upon reaching the foot of the Rockies, the men left their boat and built dugout canoes from the trunks of poplars.

The explorers hunted and fished for their food. Their daily menu was composed of deer, moose, bear, and fish. The first great event of their trip occurred in the Mandan Indian villages, where they spent the first winter. There they met a French-Canadian trapper named Toussaint Charbonneau, accompanied by his wife, Sacajawea, a young Shoshone Indian woman, and their baby. Sacajawea was happy to guide the expedition up the Missouri toward her tribal lands and to act as interpreter. Thus Lewis and Clark crossed the Rocky Mountains and followed the Columbia River to the Pacific Ocean. There the expedition spent the second winter in a makeshift fort, and in the spring started the long trip home.

During the long journey, Lewis kept a careful diary which he illustrated with accurate drawings of plants and animals. This extraordinary document tells of the landscape, climate, animals, plants, and various resources of the regions explored, as well as the customs and ways of life of the Native Americans they met. The expedition returned to St. Louis in 1806, after an absence of 25 months and 12,300 kilometers of travel. It had been an extraordinary accomplishment.

Captain Lewis watches over preparations for departure.

14

The Missouri was a difficult river to navigate, especially going upstream. At times, a towline was attached to the mast and pulled by a horse walking along the bank. The boat was used as far as the northern mountains. It was then temporarily abandoned (to be used on the return trip) and replaced by dugout canoes. The travelers carried the canoes on their shoulders through difficult crossings. During the journey, Lewis and Clark changed their habits and became men of the wilderness.

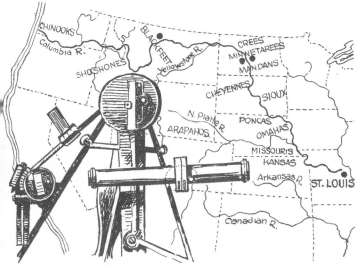

Lewis and Clark charted the regions they discovered. Beyond the Rocky Mountains, they entered the territory of the Shoshone Indians. The Indians gave them horses to reach the Columbia River, which led them to the Pacific Ocean.

All the food necessary for the expedition came from fishing and hunting. Game was bountiful everywhere. The small size of the boat did not allow the explorers to carry enough supplies for such a long voyage.

Sacajawea was of great help to the two explorers. At one point in its course, the Missouri River divides into three branches. Sacajawea, now in her native region, showed them the right direction, thus relieving them of a difficult decision. Later the young Native American was reunited with her people, now governed by her brother. In the picture below, note the fringed deerskin clothes worn by the members of the expedition. Such clothes had become the customary western dress.

The trapper and the beaver king

Fur was the first great wealth of North America and particularly of the West. French fur traders had been visiting the great forests of America even before Samuel Champlain founded Quebec in Canada in 1608. French settlers penetrated the western forests in search of the valuable fur-bearing animals, or *pelisson,* as the settlers and trappers called them. In turn, the British and later the Americans followed. Wealthy people in Europe and America wore fur not only for warmth, but also as a sign of their high social position. From 1810 to the 1830s, hat makers were particularly interested in fur. Hats made of beaver fur were the height of fashion.

From its founding, St. Louis became the capital of the fur trade. From the beginning of the 19th century, American and French trappers left St. Louis for the Rocky Mountains in order to hunt mink, muskrat, raccoon, badger, skunk, weasel, and especially beaver. The mountain man—that is, the trapper—was an extraordinary person. He spent most of his life in the high valleys and most remote canyons of the mountain ranges of western Canada and the United States. He was, in fact, fleeing civilization. He enjoyed only the unexplored wilderness. And in this great western wilderness, he met others like himself—the American Indians. He shared their life experiences and customs to such an extent that he almost became an Indian himself, even to the point of marrying an Indian woman.

Besides being a hunter, the mountain man was also a remarkably brave and resourceful explorer. He was familiar with the deserts and the vast plains as well as the mountains. His wanderings led him to the most secret places of the great West. By following the trail of the beaver, he blazed that of the pioneers. Therefore, this humble mountain man played an important role in the discovery and penetration of the wilderness.

The rough trapper meets his client, an elegant gentleman from St. Louis or New York, who wears a fine beaver hat. The beaver hat was a fashionable item in America and Europe.

Once the animal pelts were dried, they were folded and carefully compressed into bales with a rudimentary press. The trapper then loaded his horses and set out for the great yearly mountain fair, the "rendezvous."

Besides his pistol thrust into his belt and the bags containing bait and bullets, the trapper's portable gear included a hunting gun (here the famous "Hawkins rifle"), an ax or tomahawk, a hunting knife (the one here was made by "Green River"), and a trap.

Beaver, otter, raccoon, mink, or muskrat pelts—products of the hunt—were prepared at the camp during the winter. This work required a great deal of care and was usually performed by the trapper's Indian companion.

At sunset, in the waters of Rocky Mountain beaver streams, still cold as ice in the chilly mountain spring, the mountain man set his metal traps. He baited them and immersed them near the beavers' dwelling. He returned at dawn the next day to collect his catch.

Weighing about 20 kilos, with a broad, flat tail 30 centimeters long, the beaver has the most beautiful fur of all the fur-bearing animals. This explains the intense activity of trappers in North America, beginning with the French in Canada in the 17th century. French,

British, American, Spanish, and Mexican trappers hunted the beaver almost to extinction. Besides the fine quality of its fur, the beaver is an extraordinary rodent, capable of felling a small tree with its teeth in 15 minutes.

The "rendezvous," a mountain fair

Following months of wandering from one valley to another in the Rockies, the trapper arrived at the "rendezvous." This French word was used to designate a place in the mountains where each summer fur trappers and merchants from St. Louis agreed to meet to bargain over the year's catch. The rendezvous usually took place in July in a pleasant valley where, for about three weeks, there was a great market fair. Men came from all over the West, from as far away as Santa Fe and Canada, and large groups of friendly Indians also attended.

The rendezvous was also a time for exchanging news and for merrymaking, since the trappers met after months of hardship and solitude. Games, drinking bouts, wrestling matches, shooting contests, and horse and foot races took place from morning till night.

First, however, came business. Indians traded their furs for the merchants' iron tools and weapons such as knives and tomahawks; utensils such as iron kettles; and blankets, cloth, dyes, and, unfortunately, alcohol. The trappers exchanged the pelts gathered during the spring hunt for the flour, tobacco, coffee, guns and gunpowder, shot, and whiskey brought to the mountains from St. Louis by the long wagon trains of the merchants.

The great Rocky Mountain fair was over by the end of July. The mountain men took to the trails and dispersed to the far valleys for a new hunting season. When, a little later, the cold winds of autumn swept the western lands, the beaver went into hibernation, and the trappers set up their winter camps. Here the pelts were prepared and the men rested and got ready for the spring hunt.

Arrival at the rendezvous, in a green valley, was always a great pleasure for the lonely trapper.

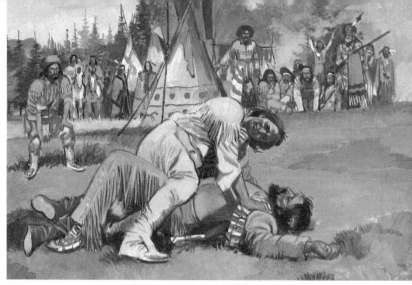

The "rendezvous" was a mountain fair. Merchants from St. Louis traded with trappers and Indians. They brought the products (good or bad) of European civilization to this natural paradise in the wilderness.

These rough and proud men met here as if at a big party. Their friendly challenges often turned into free-for-all brawls just for the fun of it. This did not, however, interfere with business, in which area the trappers drove a hard bargain.

Sometimes a trapper married an Indian woman. Her father might have exchanged her for a rifle, some glass beads, a hatchet, or alcohol. This unofficial marriage benefited the trapper, since the Indian women were skillful in preparing the animal pelts.

Mountain men and Indians sometimes competed with one another in shooting matches and in wildly dangerous horse races. Spirited dances to old Canadian or British tunes ended these violent games.

One day in the late 1830s, a man arrived in St. Louis wearing a European silk hat instead of the beaver hat which had been popular for so long. This event caused quite a stir, since it announced a change in fashion. The trappers quickly realized that the end of the prosperous fur trade was at hand. The great fur trading "empire" they had helped to build was crumbling. The rendezvous lost its purpose and disappeared. The daring and reckless mountain men became guides for wagon trains or military expeditions.

A citadel in the wilderness

Fortified trading posts. In the 1830s, there were still no white men in the West except for trappers and the occupants of forts built by the large American or (in the Northwest) British hunting and fur trading companies. These wooden citadels were built at strategic points in the immense "land of the beaver."

Although these forts were surrounded by tall log walls, they housed no military garrisons at that time. The carpenters, blacksmiths, saddlers, store-keepers, and clerks who lived there had no reason to fear the Indians. The Indians were trading partners of the "governor," as they called the local representative of the fur trading company, who directed the trading post. They periodically brought him their furs and received in exchange the same products as they had at the rendezvous. The mountain men got these same products at the fort in order to trade them, when necessary, with the Indian tribes during their wanderings.

Because of the presence of both Indians and trappers, life at the fort was always lively and interesting. Other travelers also stopped at the fort. If they happened to be important people, the "governor" received them at his own table. This official had many responsibilities, including the satisfactory transaction of the company's business and the smooth running of the trading post community.

With the decline of the fur trade toward the end of the 1830s, these strongholds in the wilderness ceased to function as trading posts. Some of them were bought by the army to shelter soldiers. Now that the conquest of the West had really begun, it was necessary to protect the great migration routes of the pioneers.

Indians arrive at Fort Laramie, the famous trading post of the 1830s, in order to exchange their furs. Between 1843 and 1860, thousands of pioneers passed by the fort.

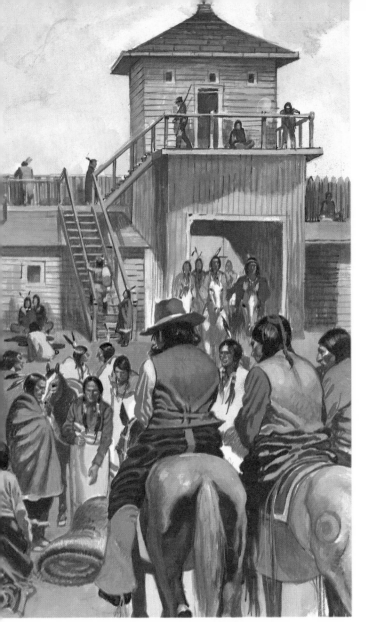

This kind of trading post belonged to a powerful company, at times employing hundreds of trappers. There were also some "free" trappers who traded directly with the Indians. There was much hard bargaining as each side sought the best deal possible.

Fort Laramie was built approximately 1,300 kilometers west of St. Louis. A single door, topped by a blockhouse sheltering a cannon, was the only opening in the log walls. As a precaution, only a few Indians at a time were admitted into the courtyard.

At the fort store, Indians exchanged their furs for the articles they desired. A buffalo skin was worth three knives or an iron kettle. A horse might be worth three to ten of these skins, depending on circumstances.

There was fierce rivalry among the Indian tribes who sought the white men as customers for their furs. One morning, one of the tribes carried out a surprise attack on a rival camp in front of Fort McKenzie on the banks of the Marias River. The fierce combat resulted in 46 deaths. Among the occupants of the fort who witnessed this battle was an artist who painted the bloody scene.

Boats for the pioneers

The "thunder canoes." After 1800, people from the East began to pour into the area between the Appalachian Mountains and the Mississippi River. Eleven states spread over this hospitable region, and increasing numbers of settlers were working their way westward. In order to reach the new lands, many of the pioneers used the rivers, since roads were few and in poor condition. To reach the Great Plains, still farther west, beaver hunters and merchants also used the rivers, particularly the Mississippi and its tributaries.

Families, animals, and goods were carried by all sorts of boats. Log rafts, flatboats, and keelboats went downstream during high water periods. These periods occurred from April to June and in the middle of winter. High water made it safer to deal with the numerous dangerous obstacles to river travel—dead trees, sandbars, tortuous passages, etc.—which marked the courses of the rivers and

made navigation difficult. Although they were quite uncomfortable, the boats were actually floating houses, and people lived on them for weeks at a time.

Thanks to the development of the steam engine, the paddle steamer, capable of moving upstream as well as down, began to appear on the rivers. By the 1830s, steamboats were helping settlers on their continual move westward. The Indians called these boats "great thunder canoes," because of the noise they made.

Steamboats belonging to the fur trading companies braved the unruly Missouri River, penetrating even deeper into the West. Sometimes these steamers carried passengers—explorers, members of scientific expeditions, or rich foreigners, who had come from Europe to "discover" the far West.

A family rides a raft downstream on the Ohio River toward the Mississippi and the West.

Roads were often limited to simple trails that were difficult to use. Rivers and streams made travel easier. Among the various vessels used was the hard-to-maneuver flatboat, which looked like a long, awkward floating box.

These riverboats sheltered their passengers for weeks during the journey. They became true houseboats, although there were no real comforts aboard. It was often necessary to share the common room with one or two animals which were stabled in a corner.

The steamboat totally changed the means of transportation. In a few years the boats became more powerful, longer (sometimes 30 to 40 meters), and even slightly more comfortable. It took the New Orleans steamboats just a few days to reach St. Louis. From there, some

The rough and carefree professional boatmen formed a small world of their own. Many of them were French Canadians. They knew the rivers thoroughly for their entire length. They knew the swiftness of their flow, their caprices, and their obstacles and dangers.

went up the Missouri River. One day, in 1832, the painter George Catlin embarked on one of these boats with his easel and palette to record scenes of the colorful western areas.

The Indians and their homes

A life in harmony with nature. The painter George Catlin spent eight years with the Indian tribes of the Great Plains. He painted their portraits, scenes of everyday life, and landscapes. Several other artists followed his example and went to various regions of the great West. Thanks to them we know something about the appearance, the conditions of life, and the customs of several tribes during the 1830s and 1840s, before the invention of photography and the massive influx of white people.

How did the Indians live in those days? East of the Mississippi, the tribes had been ruled by the settlers since the beginning of the westward migration. Broken treaties or bloody battles often deprived the Indians of their lands. Their tribes were driven back to the west bank of the Mississippi, where they tried to start over. With great courage and hard work, they succeeded. Elsewhere, in the immensities of the far West and all the way to the

Pacific coast, hundreds of tribes still lived in freedom. But for how long?

Some tribes lived by hunting and fishing, others by primitive farming. Their differing ways of life depended on the climate and physical features of their territories, as well as on their plant and animal resources. Whatever their degree of culture, these tribes could not survive unless they lived in harmony with nature. Nature supported their existence, and therefore they respected it. Earth, water, clouds, winds, plants, minerals, and animals composed a harmonious world that inspired the Indians' religious beliefs. Far from being "savages," they simply lived according to the natural rhythms that the white man's "civilization" was about to upset.

Long panels of birch bark cover the dwellings of the Ojibways, hunters and fishermen of the Great Lakes.

24

The Sioux Indians of the Great Plains lived in their tepees all year round. Twelve to fifteen poles supported the tanned buffalo skins that covered the tepee. The skins were treated and assembled by the women. Robes were made of finely worked and decorated skins.

In the Arizona desert, the Hopis built their dry stone villages, or pueblos, on high rocky plateaus called mesas. This is how they protected themselves from attack by their enemies. Crops were grown on the plain below their homes.

The Mandans were the hospitable Indians who had so warmly welcomed Lewis and Clark in the winter of 1804–1805. Their villages were built on the banks of the Missouri in what is now North Dakota. Their large round lodges were made of packed earth over wooden frames. The gently rounded roofs made good places from which to watch the colorful ceremonial dances, such as the buffalo dance shown above.

The inlets and coves of the rugged Pacific coast in the American Northwest sheltered the beautiful villages of the wealthy Haidas, the Tlingits, the Kwakiutl, and their neighbors. Extensive pine forests covered the mountain slopes of their lands. This explains the wide use of wood in the construction of their homes, their long fishing canoes, and their elaborately carved totem poles. These people were remarkable sculptors and ingenious makers of magnificent ceremonial masks.

The peaceful world of the Indian

Toward the end of the Golden Age. How many Indians were there around 1850 between the Mississippi River and the Pacific? There were probably about 350,000. Up until then, the white men were just passing through the Indian lands. The trappers, who brought along certain products of civilization, did not threaten the tribes. However, alcohol and the diseases of the "palefaces" were starting to ruin the Indians' health.

The first trains of covered wagons were no real threat either, as long as the families they transported did not settle on Indian land. Despite this foreshadowing of the white invasion, the Native Americans still pursued the way of life they had inherited from their ancestors. The Indians lived more or less comfortably, depending on the resources of their territory. The richest ones wandered and hunted on the buffalo plains. Among these were the Choctaws, whom the painter George Catlin observed playing lacrosse. This game, which originated among the Indians and which they called "baggataway," was often played between tribes. The playing field might cover a large area. The teams, which might include several hundred men each, had to throw and catch the ball with the net of a small racket, trying to keep it away from the opposing team and to get it into the opponents' goal, between two upright poles. The rules were similar to those of modern hockey, and the fights were just as rough.

For some tribes, life was more difficult. Whatever their way of life, however, the Indian tribes of the great West survived and stoically accepted their fate. But basically they lived free until the white man began arriving in increasing numbers from about 1850. This invasion of their ancestral lands would completely upset the lives of the Indian tribes. It meant the end of the Golden Age of the Indian peoples and the beginning of a long period of darkness.

Great lovers of physical sports and games, the Choctaws particularly enjoyed lacrosse.

The Apaches of Arizona lived for the most part by hunting small game. Fathers taught sons from an early age how to use the bow and arrow for hunting as well as for fighting. The lessons were useful in both cases!

The peaceful Pueblo Indians taught the Navajo women of New Mexico and Arizona how to weave. The Navajo became expert in this art, and their rugs and blankets are still famous today for their fine quality and their beauty.

The Comanches, like other American Indian tribes, acquired the horse from the Spaniards, who had conquered Mexico in the 16th century. The Comanches became formidable horsemen, bold and reckless in the hunt as well as in battle.

Kings of the northern plains, the Sioux ruled the buffalo lands. From the buffalo they obtained their food, shelter (the comfortable tepee), clothes, and many of the ordinary articles they used in their everyday life. In the picture below, the hunters have isolated several buffalo and are chasing them at a wild gallop, shooting them with bows and arrows and spearing them with lances.

Prairie Flower, a woman of the plains

A happy life in the land of the buffalo. From the time she was six years old, Prairie Flower helped her mother with the household tasks. At ten years of age, she rode a horse like a warrior, took care of Flying Cloud, her little brother, prepared pemmican (dried and pulverized buffalo meat) and the skins of small animals killed by her father and older brother. By the time she was fourteen, her practical knowledge was vast. That year she married a young brave somewhat older than she. Now she was a grown-up Indian woman with important responsibilities.

Prairie Flower set up and dismantled the family tepee during the travel from one hunting ground to another in pursuit of buffalo. With the help of her friends, she skinned the dead animals. She took pride in doing this laborious task well, and enjoyed the great feast that followed. The whole tribe had a good time eating the delicious boiled or grilled buffalo meat and drinking the warm blood. When the feast was over, Prairie Flower returned to her household chores, preparing and tanning the buffalo skins, a job that took several weeks. When this task was completed, she cut out and sewed clothes and moccasins.

Prairie Flower had four children, two boys and two girls. She loved them dearly and raised them very well with the help of her husband. The boys became brave and expert riders and hunters. The girls helped their mother, who taught them all the skills of a woman of the plains. Although her outdoor life aged her face prematurely, Prairie Flower had a long and happy life. Toward the end, she tried not to be a burden to her family or her tribe, and before she died, she thanked the Great Spirit for her happy life.

Prairie Flower lived in a tepee of the plains hunters. Everything around her reflected the wealth of the tribe, from the comfort of her dwelling and the beauty of her clothes, made of artistically decorated deerskin, to the fine construction of her son's cradle.

28

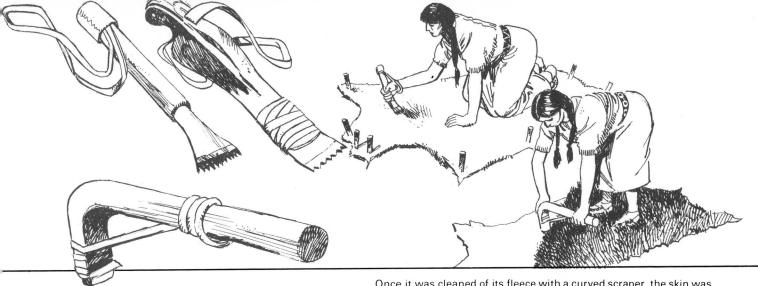

The Indian woman worked constantly. Among her many chores was the preparation of buffalo hides. This required a great deal of effort.

Once it was cleaned of its fleece with a curved scraper, the skin was turned inside out. The interior was then cleaned of its flesh and fat with special scraping tools.

Scraping the buffalo skin produced rawhide. A mixture of the animal's brain, liver, and fat was then rubbed into the skin. The same procedure was followed in preparing the skin of deer (above). The deerskin was scraped on both sides and then immersed in water.

Once removed from its bath, the skin was wrung out by vigorous twisting (background). It was then softened by rubbing it for a long period of time against a leather strip. When it dried, the skin retained its softness and suppleness.

The pole frame used in the last phase of making a buffalo robe was set up in the center of every camp. Next to it stood the rack where the strips of meat used for making pemmican were drying. Preparing the buffalo skins was a tedious and exhausting task for the women of the tribe, but it was necessary for the comfort and protection of the people during inclement weather.

On the Santa Fe trail

A profitable business. In 1821, William Becknell left from a locality on the Missouri River with four partners and some mules loaded with bundles of light merchandise. Two and a half months later, after having covered 1,250 kilometers, the small group reached Santa Fe, in what is now New Mexico. This town and its surrounding area had been part of the newly independent Mexico for several weeks. The Santa Fe area had no industry and lacked almost every kind of manufactured goods. Becknell and his companions sold their load with such profit that upon their return to Missouri, other merchants soon began to direct their wagon trains along the Santa Fe trail to this lucrative new market.

In 1822, as many as seventy American merchants arrived in Santa Fe. This is when the great Santa Fe trading trail really came into use. And it was to remain a busy trade route until the coming of the railroad to the area. The wagon trains reached Santa Fe with such merchandise as guns, glass beads, cotton, calico, muslin, cashmere, velvet, ticking, thread, buttons, scissors, files, mirrors, neckties, and gloves. On their return trip the wagons carried furs, gold, and silver. They also brought mules from Mexico and California to other areas where these animals were highly valued.

The Santa Fe wagon trains proved that in this region, unjustly called the Great American Desert, draft animals could find good pasture and wagon travel was possible. Hence, they established a bridge between the Mississippi Valley and the Southwest. Settlers followed their example and soon set out to conquer the vast wilderness.

Set on steel-banded wheels (1.75 m in diameter in the rear and 1.40 m in diameter in the front), the wagon was 7 meters long including the hitch, and 3 meters high. A wagon train included 10 to 30 vehicles.

This wagon train, starting from Franklin, Missouri, will travel 1,250 kilometers along the Santa Fe trail. Wagon trains usually moved in four parallel columns. To set up camp at night or in case of danger, the wagons would quickly form into a tight circle called a "corral." The traders and their animals in the center were well protected. Sometimes, wagon trains were attacked by Comanches or Pawnees while crossing dangerous stretches of the plains, but the occupants of the corral were generally able to beat back the Indians.

Santa Fe! After 60 to 70 days of travel, the wagon train finally sighted the town of Santa Fe. The style of its low adobe houses and the colorful customs of its inhabitants provided an exotic flavor which the travelers enjoyed after their hard journey.

Serious business generally had to wait until the day after the arrival. The first order of business for the wagon train merchants was to visit the Mexican customs office to see how much customs duties must be paid. This tax varied, but could be as high as $700 for each wagon.

Before entering the town, the travelers washed off the dust of the long, hard trail, put on clean shirts, and felt like new men. Santa Fe was rich in distractions for the newcomers—strong drink, intense gambling, and lively fandangos with beautiful señoritas.

This explains why the wagons were so heavily loaded. Goods were then displayed on the plaza in front of the governor's palace. Customers came for weeks to buy the much-needed manufactured products from the United States.

Wagons West!

A long and perilous adventure. In order to cross the "Great Desert," it was necessary to have a solid vehicle and to join a well-organized wagon train, directed by a good guide. The Conestoga wagon filled the first of these requirements. The early Conestoga wagon, built to carry freight, was a heavy wooden vehicle almost 5 meters long and about as wide as it was high (1.2 m). It was slightly raised at both ends to prevent the shifting of the freight it carried. It looked like a boat whose hull, often painted blue, was perched on high, sturdy wheels banded with steel. A white canvas cover resting on arches completed the picture. Later Conestoga wagons, built to carry families and their meager possessions, had lower sides and bigger canvas tops. These "prairie schooners" were pulled by peaceful oxen or by mules. The convoy might include 30 to 100 wagons, depending on the year and the destination.

Families wishing to move west would assemble at a previously designated place in early spring, and there make arrangements for the trip. Companies were formed, and guides—often former fur trappers—were selected. With the arrival of suitable weather conditions, the wagon train would start out.

A convoy of this type broke camp at 7 A.M. Whips cracked. A bugle called to order the arrangement of the front wagons, behind which the others lined up. The guide and captain, supreme commander, galloped all along this column to check the order and give advice. He then went to the front and cried out, "Wagons West!"

Thus began the long journey, during which men, women, and children pursued the dream of the promised land. Many of them never made their destination, having died of disease, been killed by the Indians, or simply having turned back, discouraged by the hard trip. For the others, once the obstacles were overcome, the West offered the chance of a new life 3,000 kilometers away from their starting point, under different skies.

The signal is given and the adventure begins. The brave pioneers start out for the great West beyond the horizon.

The covered wagon was the forerunner of our trailers or mobile homes. It carried families and their dreams across plains, over mountains, and through deserts for four to five months. Imagine what it must have been like to live aboard this long, bumpy box!

The entire family crowded, more or less comfortably, under the frail white canvas of this rolling house. The family wagon also carried a few pieces of furniture, some farming tools, mattresses, and food. Life was full of anxiety until the goal was reached.

Rivers were crossed at known points during low summer waters. Routes and timetables had to be carefully followed. At times there were unexpected events, such as a sudden flood, when wagons

might be carried away and animals drowned. Occasionally people had to lighten their wagons, leaving some of their precious possessions along the trail. This was a disaster feared by all.

Every night when they stopped, the wagons formed a circle inside which was a bustle of activity. To the children fell the task of gathering firewood. The women prepared the evening meal while the men tended the animals and repaired the wagons.

Intense heat, devastating tornadoes, meager pastures, dried-up water holes, and steep mountain passes impeded the progress of the wagon trains. Not the least of their problems were Indian attacks, which were a real but infrequent danger.

San Francisco, the gold capital

Gold in California! On January 24, 1848, a blacksmith named James W. Marshall discovered gold nuggets at the bottom of a stream in the foothills of the Sierra Nevada, a mountain range 100 kilometers northwest of San Francisco Bay. By 1849 the news had spread throughout the world, and 30,000 immigrants changed the quiet town of San Francisco, with less than 2,000 inhabitants, into a colorful, animated, and picturesque tower of Babel.

Within a few weeks, Kanakas from Hawaii, blacks from the American South, Chinese, Peruvians, Mexicans, Canadians, and Europeans were converging on San Francisco from the four corners of the earth. Some disembarked from the great trans-Pacific sailing ships, while others crossed the Atlantic and rounded Cape Horn. (The Panama Canal was not opened until 1914.) Still others came across the continent. Many of these newcomers took to the mountains, but others remained in town. And what a town! It was a labyrinth of tents, wooden shacks, and various shelters, which burned down a total of six times in eighteen months. Few towns have ever seen such a collection of scoundrels, thieves, adventurers of all sorts, bandits, and criminals.

To fight against them and against crime in general, the peaceful citizens of San Francisco formed vigilante committees and decided to take matters into their own hands. Their justice was swift and merciless. Little by little, however, law and order triumphed.

In a few years, real houses sprang up, the rich built themselves fine homes, and luxurious hotels and restaurants opened their doors. By 1859, San Francisco had almost 100,000 inhabitants and was the "gold capital," and one of the richest cities in America.

A ship docks in San Francisco. Its crew deserts to go to search for gold!

In 1848, San Francisco was a quiet town of no more than 2,000 people. By the end of 1849, it already had 30,000 inhabitants living in all types of shelters—shanties, wooden cabins, tents, etc. The housing shortage was such that some big abandoned sailing ships were pulled up onto the shores of the bay and turned into living quarters. One of them even became San Francisco's first prison and was said to be always full. A year later, gas and water were installed in the city.

In 1852, there were over 20,000 Chinese in America. Many of them worked in the gold mines of the Sierra Nevada. They lived in ethnic neighborhoods called "Chinatowns." A great number became cooks and servants. Most did the harshest, most back-breaking drudgery.

At the beginning of the gold rush, there was little law and order in San Francisco or in the mining camps. Citizens took justice into their own hands by forming vigilante committees that hanged thieves and murderers on the spot.

The saloons of the town became more prosperous than the gold prospectors themselves. One could meet there a strange international clientele who often spent in one day the gold dust obtained from several months' hard work.

During the first few months of San Francisco's existence as a "gold town," mud drowned the new streets. One of the many jokes of the time was about a man on his mule who sank into the mud completely, and only his hat marked the place where he once had been.

Henri Chatillon, prospector

The real gold mine is not always the one you expect. In the port city of Le Havre in France, Henri Chatillon boarded a sailing ship bound for New York. At New York, he boarded another ship, loaded with emigrants, which was bound for San Francisco by way of Cape Horn. Three months later, Chatillon arrived in San Francisco, where he met other Frenchmen. (Many people called the French newcomers "Keskydees," because, unable to understand the languages spoken in this new country, they kept asking, "*Qu'est-ce qu-il dit?*"—"What is he saying?"

Chatillon joined some of his fellow Frenchmen who were planning to go out to the gold mines. They dressed themselves like Californians, with flannel shirts, pants of thick brown cloth tucked into sturdy leather boots, and large-brimmed hats. They bought tools—picks, shovels, and pans—and provisions, and left for a gold mine camp called Jesus Maria, in the Sierras. People said there were rich gold-bearing deposits on the banks of the stream there. The camp itself was a depressing sight, with its shacks of boards or logs and its tents perched precariously on the slopes of a gorge.

Chatillon and his companions quickly realized that Jesus Maria was an extremely uncomfortable and wretched place. The cold and snow made the winters particularly unbearable. For three years they led a hard-working life, devoid of almost all pleasures. Finally, tired of this disappointing and exhausting life, Chatillon abandoned his claim and returned to San Francisco. During his absence, the city had become much improved, and he decided to settle there. Having been a cook in France at one time, he opened a restaurant featuring "specialties of Paris." This turned out to be his real gold mine!

In new clothes and with hope in their hearts, Henry Chatillon and his companions discover the Sierra Nevada.

A prospector puts his pan full of dirt that he thinks may contain gold into a stream. He moves the pan in circles and the gravel and sand are washed away, leaving—if he is lucky—the heavier gold dust behind on the bottom of the pan.

The "arrastra" was a mill used by Mexican miners. Large stones pulled by a horse crushed the gold ore, thus freeing the precious nuggets. Steam-driven mechanical crushers were much more efficient and convenient.

Easier and more efficient to use than a "washing pan" was a sluice. The dirt was put into one end of an oblong wooden box and water was passed through, washing away the sand and gravel. The gold dust or nuggets were retained at the bottom of the sluice.

In 1846, there were fewer than 20,000 people, other than Indians, living in all of California. By 1850, California's population had reached almost 100,000. However, less than 10 percent of the people drawn to California by the hope of gold were women. There were practically no women at all in the boisterous mining camps. The picture below shows the prospectors dancing with each other.

The stagecoach era

Traveling by stage. Every prospector returning from the mines of California, with or without his fortune, praised the Wells Fargo Company, which came to San Francisco in 1852. Its fast stagecoaches were drawn by four horses and driven by bold and expert drivers. They carried passengers and mail to the most remote gold mining camps in all weather and on all kinds of roads.

The stagecoaches of John Butterfield and, a bit later, those of Ben Holladay, were the first transcontinental coaches. Butterfield's southern route covered 4,500 kilometers from Tipton, Missouri, to the gold capital, San Francisco, and included 200 stations.

Butterfield employed a thousand salaried hands, and directed a large fleet of coaches, among which were 250 of the celebrated "Concords." These red or green painted vehicles were the most elegant of all the stagecoaches, and certainly the most comfortable, being suspended on thick leather straps which served as shock absorbers. These coaches could carry as many as 21 passengers, most of them on the roof.

The Concords were used at the beginning and at the end of the long journey. Lighter express wagons were used for the rougher portions of the route. These were smaller and faster, and built low to the ground so that they were not likely to be upset, but they were far less comfortable than the Concords.

Among the hazards of stagecoach travel were the possibilities of overturning, being stuck fast in mud or snow, and breaking down. Coaches were also subject to Indian attacks and to holdups by robbers.

Butterfield's coaches, and then those of Ben Holladay, linked Missouri to the Pacific in a maximum of 23 to 25 days. But the stage lines could not really compete with the railroads, which by 1869 spanned the continent.

The stagecoach is about to leave Missouri for California—a long and uncomfortable 25-day trip.

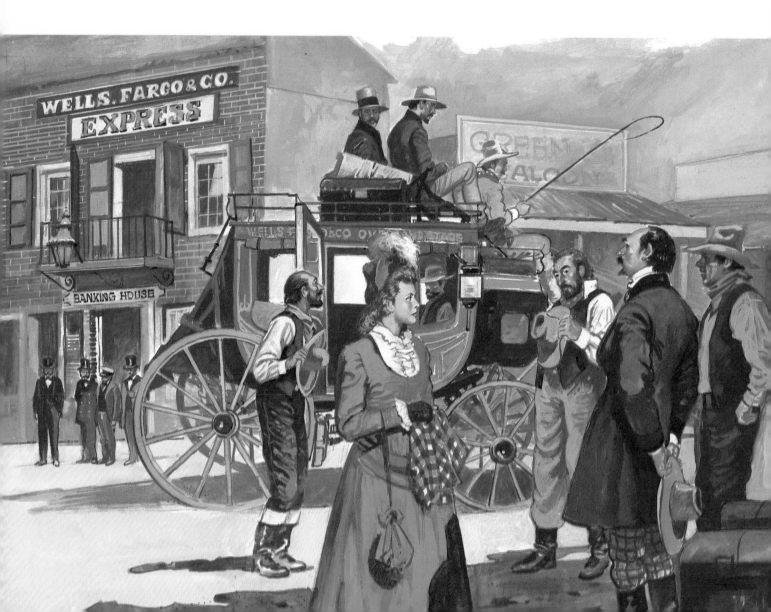

An armed guard always accompanied the driver while crossing unsafe territory. One driver was relieved by another about every 80 kilometers. The stagecoach traveled at speeds of 7 to 25 kilometers an hour depending on the terrain.

The inside of the coach held six to nine passengers, depending on the model. Some coaches, such as the Concord, could also accommodate passengers on the top deck. Each passenger was allowed a maximum of 20 kilos of luggage and payed $200 for the whole trip.

It took 10 minutes to change horses at the "swing stations," which were about 20 kilometers apart. "Home stations" were about 80 kilometers apart. Here drivers were changed and passengers might stop for a short while to eat some bacon or pork, perhaps some potatoes or beans, and drink muddy black coffee. If a passenger had to stay overnight in a home station, which usually was primitive and dirty, he would have to sleep on the earth floor because bunks were reserved for employees of the line.

Indian attacks were rarer than the holdups by bandits so frequently shown in "western" movies. But in February 1861, Chief Cochise of the Chiricahua Apaches, who had recently been wrongly accused of a kidnapping by an American army officer, attacked a Butterfield coach at Apache Pass, Arizona, killing the driver and his assistant and precipitating a long Indian war.

The winged horses of the Pony Express

The greatest horse race in the world! Ten days to cross from Saint Joseph, Missouri, to San Francisco, California, 3,145 kilometers in each direction! Such were the daily exploits of the young riders of the Pony Express. In 1860 and 1861 these 15- to 25-year-old men carried 9 kilograms of mail on thin paper secured in the four pockets of leather saddlebags called *mochilas*. Day and night, no matter what the terrain or weather, rain or shine, summer and winter, they galloped at full speed on strong, sure-footed Indian horses.

Home stations at about 50-kilometer intervals and swing stations at 15-kilometer intervals dotted the route. Most of them were mere stables, kept by a watchman and one or two stablemen. Struggling against the clock, each rider covered a daily distance of about 60 to 120 kilometers, depending on the terrain. Sometimes, for unforeseen reasons, some of these experienced riders had to double or triple the distance normally covered. This was the case of young William Frederick Cody, the future Buffalo Bill, fifteen years old at the time. He broke all records by riding 531 kilometers without any rest. This exploit made him famous.

The bravery and boldness of its riders, as well as the exceptional nature of its performance, earned the Pony Express its international fame. The prowess of its messengers was admired even in Europe. Unfortunately, after only eighteen months the Pony Express went bankrupt. The service cost much more to operate than could be charged for the letters that were carried. And the newly completed transcontinental telegraph line could carry messages faster than the swift horses and their daring riders. The horses remained in their stables and the riders were let go. All that was left to them was the glory of having covered a distance equivalent to 24 times around the earth and having carried 34,753 letters in 308 round trips.

The mission of the Pony Express rider was to get the mail through at any cost.

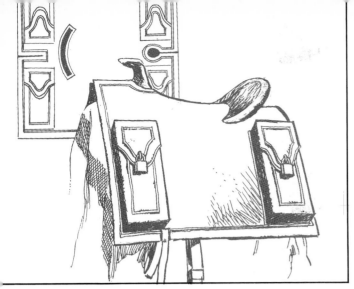

Before the rider left, the overseer locked each of the pockets of the leather mochila. Upon arriving in San Francisco, California, or in Saint Joseph, Missouri, the bureau chief opened the bags with an identical key.

Builders of the first telegraph line across the western United States followed the route of the Pony Express. The first message was sent over the line from San Francisco to Washington, D.C., on October 24, 1861. The Indians called the telegraph the "talking wire."

April 13, 1860: the first rider of the Pony Express arrived in Sacramento, California, at nightfall. The whole town awaited him on the main street, which was lit with bonfires. The municipal band accompanied the town officials, who welcomed the intrepid rider.

It took only a few seconds to change horse and rider at each relay station. The Pony Express always struggled against the clock, day and night. Men and animals performed wonders in this enormous undertaking.

Shortly after his arrival, during the ovations, the brave messenger boarded a steamboat which took him down the Sacramento River to San Francisco. The mail had just traveled from the Missouri River to the Pacific Ocean in a record time of ten days.

The victory of the "iron horse"

New York to San Francisco in seven days! Construction of the transcontinental railroad linking the center of the continent to the Pacific coast began in 1863. Though the building of the railroad was authorized by an act of Congress in 1862, construction was not really in full swing until after the Civil War ended in 1865. Two companies were created—the Central Pacific started in California and worked toward the East; the Union Pacific started at the Missouri River and worked in the opposite direction. In this gigantic undertaking, men had to conquer the plains, the mountains, and the high plateaus; brave enormous distances; overcome terrible obstacles; and face all kinds of weather in the changing seasons for 2,800 kilometers.

Thousands of workers participated in this project, including a great number of Irish and Chinese immigrants. The former came from the East and worked on the Union Pacific side; the latter came from San Francisco and worked for the Central Pacific. They lived in camps of tents and barracks that followed them as work on the line progressed. Well-organized teams fought against time. They had to work fast. In the mountains, the Chinese used a powerful explosive, nitroglycerin, for the first time, to blast away rocks. Thousands of Chinese laborers worked on the most difficult and precipitous sections of the future Central Pacific roadbed. On their side, the Irish workmen of the Union Pacific were often attacked by the Plains Indians. Due to this danger, a military escort had to be assigned to each team.

Despite all these inconveniences, both lines progressed toward each other and met on May 10, 1869. On May 15, the first train ran between Chicago and Sacramento. Ten years later, daily trains were traveling in both directions. Now it took seven days to go from New York to San Francisco. What an improvement over the stagecoaches!

Chinese workers cut a railroad pass through rock in the difficult Sierra Nevada.

Work gangs of 20 men laid ties and rails and hammered in the spikes. The Union Pacific workers had to bring wood for ties from the distant forests of the North and East to the treeless plains. The Central Pacific workers had to build long wooden galleries in the Sierra Nevada to protect the road from winter snows. A thousand obstacles delayed the progress of both lines. And yet, they made it.

It took three blows of a sledge hammer for the workers to drive in a steel rail spike. They used 50 spikes per rail and 400 rails per 1,600 meters of track. Track gauge was set at 1.41 meters. It was wider than that used in Europe.

On May 10, 1869, at Promontory Point, Utah, near the Great Salt Lake, the two tracks finally met. The presidents of the companies clumsily drove in the last three gold and silver spikes while the soldiers presented arms. The telegraph announced the news to all of

The first transcontinental trains burned wood. The stoker continuously fed logs into the firebox in order to obtain a speed of 30 to 40 kilometers an hour. The slightest hill slowed the locomotive. At times, outlaws took advantage of this.

America, then to the world. This moment was an important historical event, as extraordinary as the landing of the first man on the moon. The Union Pacific laid 1,740 km of rail and the Central Pacific laid 1,100 km.

The surprises of a trip by train

A very lively trip. One day, Harry Thedeum Davis, a wealthy Chicago businessman, took the transcontinental railroad to visit his brother in Sacramento, California.

The trip was enchanting up to the Missouri River, thanks to the comfort of the beds in the sleeping cars, invented by George Pullman, and the quality of the food in the dining cars, also designed by the Pullman Palace Car Company. Harry Davis was impressed by the vast loneliness of the plains through which the Union Pacific train dragged along at 40 kilometers per hour. The monotony of this portion of the trip was, however, interrupted by a series of incidents which Harry T. Davis had believed up to this time to be imaginary.

First of all, during the crossing of the plains, the train stopped. Two young masked bandits with big hats burst into the dining car at mealtime. They threatened the travelers with guns and politely relieved them of their money, watches, and jewelry. The next day, in Wyoming, the train had to stop for several hours until a large herd of buffalo crossed the track. Some passengers armed with Winchesters shot a few of them for fun.

When he arrived in Sacramento, Harry, with his heart pounding, told his brother about the thrilling events of his trip. He was especially excited about an Indian attack on the train. This, he told his brother, had scared him to death, and his courage did not return until the Indians had galloped away.

Upon his return to Chicago, he found his wife waiting for him at the station. "What a trip!" he said with enthusiasm and a new air of importance. "I must tell you about my adventures; they really made all the difficulties seem worthwhile!"

Harry Thedeum Davis boards the train for Sacramento.

44

Two young men show up in the dining car with guns in hand. Once they have left, people whisper the names of Frank and Jesse James, the famous bandits. They robbed the passengers and the mail safe of about $12,000.

Suddenly the train stops in open country. Two of Harry's traveling companions load their Winchesters and shoot out through the windows. What are they aiming at? Harry looks out, and sees a herd of buffalo.

Harry cannot believe his eyes! Hundreds of buffalo surround the train, which is forced to stop. Placid, indifferent to the "iron horse," the heavy mammals cross the track for two long hours. Harry thinks he must be dreaming. When the train finally starts again, one of the travelers swears that the month before, he had to wait two days for the same thing. There were tens of thousands of buffalo. And his story was true!

Two days later, a new alert—Indians. Harry T. Davis thought his last hour had come. He ventured a timid glance out the window and saw the feather-bonneted warriors. They were galloping along the track as if to race with the train. What would happen if their arrows or bullets hit the fireman or the engineer?

Cowboys and longhorns

A rough profession. Despite himself, the cowboy has become a legendary figure, popularized by stories, "western" movies, and television. In reality, he was simply a hard worker. Between 1860 and 1890, he labored painfully in the great pastures of the American plains from Texas to Montana. In this vast area, cattle were raised to supply meat to the large cities in the East, from Chicago to New York. The cattle lived outdoors all year round, on ranches sometimes as large as 2,500 square kilometers.

During the cattle drives, herds of bellowing animals moved along the trails, tended by teams of fifteen to twenty cowboys. The cowboys rode in front, behind, and on the sides of the herd. Those who rode behind the herd swallowed clouds of choking dust kicked up by the "longhorns." Moving 3,000 or 4,000 of these animals across the prairies from the ranches to the railroads in Kansas often proved to be a trying experience for the men. They traveled through arid plains, crossed rivers, endured the scorching sun and torrential rains, fought back sleep during night watches, and risked their lives during wild stampedes. Who would have lightly chosen such an exhausting life under these conditions? Very few people.

The time came when the "man of the saddle" saw the arrival of the "man of the plow"—that is, the farmer—in his territory. There was friction between these two groups—the cattlemen and the farmers. The farmers fenced in their lands with barbed wire, thus cutting off the cattle trails and restricting the freedom of the cowboy. Eventually the cowboy realized and came to accept that the great days of the cattle kingdom had come to an end. However, history and legend were awaiting him; and there he still gallops freely.

A working arena—the corral

The cowboy enjoyed beef stew, red beans and salt pork, pancakes, and pies. To the cowboys, the cook was the most valuable man of the whole team. Meals were the only moments of relaxation during work on the ranch.

At the spring and fall roundups, cowboys branded the young cattle. Each ranch owner had his own brand. It allowed him to recognize his animals, which roamed freely all year round in the grazing areas, when it was time to send them to market.

Cowboys led herds of 3,000 to 4,000 animals over 800 to 1,000 kilometers of dangerous trails, from the Texas ranches to the railroad in Kansas. This trip required three months of continuous work. It was the most important event of the year.

Upon arriving in town, the cowboys relaxed in a manner that was often rather exuberant, since most of them were young and full of energy. They had three months' salary from the cattle drive in their pockets and felt rich. They frequented the saloons, and when they became boisterous and

sometimes dangerous, the sheriff (the man with the tin star) did not always have the upper hand. However, when things got out of hand, he did not hesitate to intervene and lock up the culprits in the town jail.

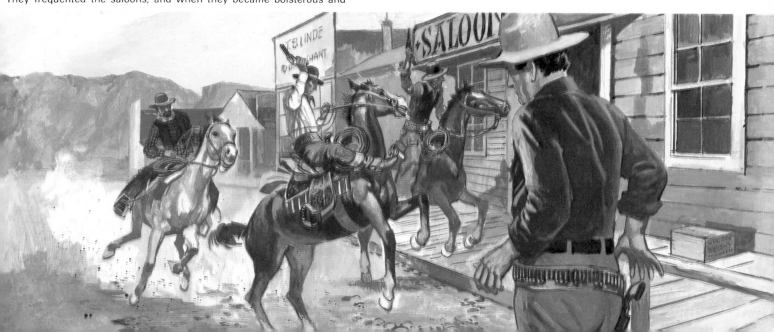

"We, the farmers of the plains. . ."

The breadbasket of America. The government made land grants at very advantageous terms. Nevertheless, interested people hesitated for a long time before venturing into the inhospitable north central plains. Trees had to be planted and the land irrigated. Brave pioneers accepted the challenge and the railroads brought them there.

Many of them were greatly disappointed and disturbed by the monotony of the landscape. Once they had sheltered their families as well as possible, the men began to work the land. Although their tools were primitive and their work animals not particularly sturdy, the pioneers worked tenaciously. They managed to produce harvests of wheat or corn. But a good harvest required a great deal of luck, for summer droughts might unrelentingly scorch the fields, sudden prairie fires could destroy the crops, violent winds often dried up the plants, and some years millions of locusts ate everything in sight.

The early years were a very painful period for the farmers. Some of them grew tired of all the obstacles and returned to the cities. However, the majority persevered. They often had to mortgage their farms at very heavy interest rates. In general, income did not cover expenses. And the railroads charged high rates for shipping the farmers' crops back East.

Gradually the situation improved. Farmers learned ways of farming that were better suited to the land and climate. Better kinds of seeds were used. Crops became more abundant. The federal government made laws to control the rates the railroads could charge. The toil of the farmers was rewarded by increasing profits. Slowly they transformed the Great Plains into the "breadbasket" of America.

"Today my father plowed the first furrow on our land. . ."

"We lived in a treeless region on the Kansas plains. We built our house with sod, the only material available. A mound of earth and grass protected it from the winds. This is a photograph of our entire family. I am on the swing."

"We used buffalo manure to heat our house, since it was the only thing around that would burn. My mother was exhausted from gathering it. I admired her courage and energy; she worked constantly, for our lives depended on it."

"Our primitive home barely sheltered us from the elements, which were often violent. Despite their misery, my parents were never discouraged. Following their example, I developed the willpower necessary to build the future. And I always remained hopeful."

"Miss Betsy, our teacher, was fond of us. She was as poor as we were. I remember our sod schoolhouse, covered with green grass in the spring. There I learned reading, writing, and arithmetic. We loved Miss Betsy."

"The years passed. My parents took advantage of new laws allowing us to increase our land holdings. We moved to a different region and finally found good land. Our new neighbors helped my father build a more comfortable house. Advances in technology brought us new machinery with which we, the farmers, were proud to harvest the rich crops of the Great Plains, our vast home."

Soldiers in the West

A dull life. Starting in the 1870s, the American government built dozens of forts in the West in order to protect the trails threatened by rebellious Indians. Each of these forts housed a garrison of 50 to 200 men.

The fort consisted simply of a series of buildings surrounding a large central exercise yard. The picturesque log-fenced trading posts that flourished in the days of the trappers had disappeared.

The soldier's life was no fun inside these barracks, isolated in the western wilderness. He enlisted for three to five years, often because he could not find work in the East, or sometimes simply because he sought adventure. His monthly salary was only $16. Life was dull, often devoid of heroism or valor, and consisted of assemblies, chores, exercises, inspections, and the construction of roads.

Many soldiers never saw a single Indian. But to other soldiers the Indian showed himself to be a truly fierce enemy, and for good reason. Settlers occupied his lands, establishing ranches and farms with little concern for the treaties the government had made with the Indians. White hunters killed the buffalo the Indians depended on, first to provide food for the railroad building crews, and later, in ever increasing numbers, so that their hides, meat, or tongues might be sent back East. When the exasperated tribes launched guerilla attacks against the usurpers, the white men called in the army. So the soldier left his camp and wore himself out pursuing the Indians, whom he sometimes faced in deadly ambushes or bloody skirmishes.

In pursuing the Indians, many recruits saw their first action—and, at times, their last. On June 25, 1876, an ambush by the Sioux Indians near the Little Bighorn River in Montana cost the lives of 265 soldiers and their commander, General George Armstrong Custer. This was a resounding defeat in the history of the far West.

Morning assembly at a western fort

Army life was not romantic, especially when the sergeant carefully inspected the arms. The sergeant was a brawler who, with threats of punishment, was single-handedly able to terrorize a company of 50 men.

The Gatling gun was a very elaborate weapon. Its gunner turned a crank, which rotated the barrels. For a brief moment, each one was positioned in front of the firing chamber containing the bullets. The Gatling gun could fire hundreds of times each minute.

Some of the cavalry officers in the western armies were totally inexperienced. Others were skilled in Indian warfare. They knew how to use the information supplied by the Indian scouts, who were valuable aides.

The western army often clashed with the Indians, who were enraged at forts being built on Indian territory. Moreover, the white settlers and miners did not respect the treaties their government had signed. In anger the Indians struck out against the settlers and others who

Maneuvers, patrols, or campaigns against the Indians drew the soldiers away from the fort. This was the military life, with adventure and sometimes even danger. But does one think of danger when relaxing over a meal?

killed their food—the buffalo—and took their land. In retaliation, the soldiers massacred the Indians. Thus the fury of the Sioux, Comanches, Kiowas, and Apaches was unleashed against the soldiers, who paid a heavy price for the "taming of the West."

Birth of a boom town

A mad race. Toward the end of the 19th century, the American government allowed the whites to settle in vast portions of the Indian territories in the state today known as Oklahoma. This Indian name means "the land of the red people." This land had been set aside for the Indians by the American government, and many tribes driven west of the Mississippi River by the advancing white settlers had settled there between 1830 and 1840. This Indian territory sheltered several Indian nations, each in a specific region. They all managed to live more or less happily together.

However, toward the end of the 1800s, they were threatened by a new danger. A law passed in 1887 declared that the head of each Indian family could possess no more than 64 hectares of land. Also, the family had to engage in farming or cattle raising. Besides obliging the nomadic Indian to change to a sedentary way of life, this law considerably reduced his land and freed tens of thousands of hectares for the white settlers.

Then in 1889, President Benjamin Harrison declared that the Oklahoma District of the Indian territories would be opened to settlers exactly at noon on April 22, 1889. Prospective settlers gathered at the boundary as if at a race, ready to rush in and stake their claim. At the appointed time, the craziest race that ever took place under western skies began, and by nightfall over a million acres had been claimed. This is how the cities of Guthrie and Oklahoma City were born. Guthrie was born in just one day—a tent city with 10,000 inhabitants.

In 1907 Oklahoma became a state. Most Indians adapted reasonably well to the white population, which by 1910 had grown to 1,657,155 inhabitants.

Ready, set, go! The craziest race in the history of the West is about to start.

Each person had to choose his land at a glance. First come, first served. Then the land had to be staked out. Five years later the land would officially become the property of the first occupant.

Men and women on horseback surged ahead of the mass of vehicles of all kinds. Some women showed unbelievable energy and courage. They all galloped at full speed toward the plots on which they wished to build their homes.

The town of Guthrie, Oklahoma, was born, with a population of 10,000, in one day, on April 22, 1889. Still more settlers arrived the next day. The original area soon had to be increased fourfold. The first land office was located in a tent. This is where the landowners came

At first, tents were pitched on the land of the future cities. Then wooden buildings were erected. Long wagon trains made many trips to bring the necessary lumber and other materials to this treeless area. In a few weeks, a city began to take shape.

to register their land. William Wrigley, the inventor of chewing gum, built his factory close by. In 1890 Guthrie became the capital of Oklahoma. However, in 1910 the capital was moved to Oklahoma City.

The new West

A fantastic adventure was about to end. At the end of the 19th century, the West was definitively tamed. A whole new population now lived between the Mississippi Valley and the Pacific coast. There still remained wide open spaces, but the best land was taken. The long march of the pioneers toward the sunset had ended.

This adventure was a vivid example of the inexhaustible energy of the American people. On the other hand, it also ruined the Indians, who were now confined to poor reservations. In 1900, approximately 250,000 of them lived in misery. Their former lands were now the sites of cities, huge cattle ranches, and cultivated fields. Roads and railways crisscrossed the continent.

The people of this new West worked very hard. New inventions in tools and machinery enabled the settlers to increase the yield of their lands. However, men and women were still preoccupied by the hardships of everyday life, a life that was slowly growing a little easier. Even though there was still poverty in certain regions, there was always hope to escape from it one day.

In spite of their lives of hard work and poverty, people took the time to enjoy themselves. They gathered together in family groups and with their neighbors. They celebrated religious holidays and attended agricultural shows. They started to become sports fans—fans of baseball, bicycle races, athletic competitions, etc. The daring skills of the rodeo champions excited the crowds. Cowboys were kings, and a real myth was being born.

"Buffalo Bill" Cody staged a lively version of life in the old West in the arena of his show—with Indians, cowboys who were trick riders and excellent marksmen, and even stagecoaches. At the same time, Thomas Alva Edison invented movies. Among the most popular early movies were westerns, of course, in which the dream of the wide open spaces was renewed.

Like his blood brothers, Quanah Parker, the last of the Comanche chiefs, lived through two periods—before and after the conquest of the West.

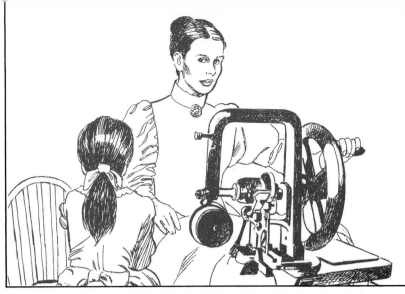

In the last half of the 19th century, oil made Texas and then Oklahoma rich. This was the time of the rush for "black gold." Soon forests of derricks limited the horizon of the cowboy, who was deprived of the wide open spaces.

The department stores of the cities in the East shipped their catalogs to farmers' wives. These women then began to set up their households with the latest items that progress had to offer. Life improved as the 19th century was drawing to a close.

Strange meetings took place on country roads in the West at the turn of the century—progress came face to face with the past. The humble covered wagon, headed for extinction or for a museum, was a reminder of the saga that had ended. The automobile, the symbol of

modern times, heralded the birth of modern America. Only half a century separated these two vehicles. Though each was indicative of a different time and social condition, they both represented the American people, on the move toward a better life.

The West left the world its legend composed of memories shared by a whole new people. It was naively but attractively revived in the "Wild West Show" of William Frederick Cody, popularly known as Buffalo

Bill. From 1883 to 1917 (the year of his death), Buffalo Bill's Wild West Show traveled through America and Europe, and was presented to millions of spectators.

Travel Notes

1838–1872

Billy McPlumcott was born in 1821 to a French mother and an Irish father. At first he was a trapper, then cowboy, prospector, scout for the Texas Rangers, journalist, and finally tramp printer. He died in a Cheyenne ambush while accompanying a wagon train from Wyoming to Montana. During his travels he kept daily notes of his experiences, which he used to write the articles he sent to numerous newspapers for whom he worked—the *Territorial Enterprise,* the *Nugget,* the *Arizona Kicks,* and the *Kansas Courier,* among others.

April 15, 1849

I have decided to go West as George Catlin did in 1832. This former lawyer wandered among the Indian tribes to paint portraits of their chiefs. . . .

The Sioux are wellknown horse thieves. One of their favorite pastimes is to steal from the neighboring tribes. The young braves are especially expert at this, trading the horses for a wife once they decide to marry. These horses are generally small. Three hundred years in the wild have managed to transform the magnificent mounts of the Spanish conquerors into flea-bitten piebald nags. The most reputable ones, the Appaloosas, are selected by the Nez Perces of Oregon. In their language, "appaloosa" means "the best."

The Indians believe that their horses understand their language. When they think their horses are responsible for a victory, they offer them an eagle's feather as a reward for their courage and valor. At the age of fourteen, the young Comanche brave sets out alone on foot to capture his first horse. For days and nights he stalks the herd of mustangs in which he has already sighted the mount he wants, until he finally goes near it, caresses it, and manages to bridle it.

Thousands of these mustangs frolic on the plains. The Indians use them to replenish their cavalry, but the capture of a horse is not left to chance. Sometimes the animal is observed for years; the Indian knows the quality of the mare and the wild stallion who sired it. This is why the Indian ponies, which are carefully selected from among the most rapid and enduring ones, regularly outrun the white men's horses.

Before the arrival of the horse in America, the Indians traveled on foot, and dogs pulled their "travois," a sort of

triangular sled upon which their belongings were placed when moving camp. There are always many dogs around their villages. These animals bark a lot and cannot be approached. Without a doubt, they know they had better not be caught by men since, when the Indian wants to show his friendship for his guest, he serves him boiled dog accompanied by a sauce of prairie herbs and wild turnips. Every dog that scurries to greet a visitor is sure to be sacrificed in his honor.

The Thal-Tan Indians of Upper Canada have a race of dogs that are stocky, with thick fur and a thick tail.[1] They use them to hunt bear, lynx, and porcupines. Another tribe of Indians have a sort of basset hound used to chase the beaver out of its dwelling.

[1] The Thal-Tan bear dog still exists, but it is difficult to raise, and every attempt to breed it outside of its native land has ended in failure.

May 25, 1868

We are about to leave the Red River valley for Kansas with a herd of 6,500 longhorns that crazy Bill Wesley claims he will then be able to drive to the Dakota territory. I wonder how this adventure will end, since we have no federal license to cross the Indian territories of Oklahoma. The cowboys who

are with us look more like stagecoach robbers than honest men, but we'll probably be glad to have them with us when we face the Cheyennes, Arapahos, and Comanches whose hunting grounds we'll cross. . . .

This spring's roundup lasted six weeks, and all this time was needed to sort out these wretched beasts and get them on the trail. Longlegged and looking still thinner because of their long horns (sometimes over a yard in length), these animals are the descendants of beasts introduced by the Spaniards and then allowed to return to the wild state. The Texans have taken the best part of these. They are shipping them to Chicago, St. Louis, and even New York, but the shrewdest of them are selling the cattle to farmers going West. Many of ours are full of ticks, a probable sign of Texas fever, but we'll probably sell them for three or four dollars a head. The losses we'll bear en route will hardly affect Bill's wallet. . . .

Salted and smoked pork, beans, and peas—this is our menu for many weeks. It is out of the question to slaughter a cow along the way, unless it breaks a leg. Too bad! Sliced, rolled in flour, and sauteed in kidney fat, the meat of these longhorns becomes more or less edible. Anyway, I noticed some Irish people among the emigrants who are with us, and should the occasion arise, we will try to use the unwanted top ribs for an Irish stew like in the old country. And then, there will be hunting . . . if the Indians allow us the time! . . .

July 1868

As we head toward the Northwest, the grass is becoming thicker and more beautiful. We advance slowly to allow the cattle to take advantage of it; we cover 10 to 15 miles a day. Up till now, there has been very little loss. The cowboys stand guard to warn us of attacks by Indians and wolves. We often see packs of wolves roaming around the herd. They are very big, weighing 125 to 150 pounds, and much more cunning than the coyotes. Each cowboy has five to six horses at his disposal. Our convoy includes about a hundred unmounted horses. They form a column which stays in the rear, surrounded by some Texans, who do not care much for the work that is being forced upon them by their boss.

CENTRE CULTUREL AMÉRICAIN

July 23

Toward evening, at the top of a hill, we are suddenly greeted by a spectacle that strikes even the oldest among us. The whole plain, as far as the eye can see, is covered by an enormous mass of buffalo. Our field extends over a length of at least 10 miles and a width of 8 miles, and in this entire space there is not one single clearing in this countless multitude. . . .

We have to wait three days for the herd to disappear over the horizon, but as the saying goes, "where you find the buffalo, you find the Indian"; 100 to 200 Cheyennes are in hot pursuit and pay no attention to us. Thank God, the boss knew they would be right behind the buffalo and expressly forbade the Texans from shooting at the animals. . . .

August 1868

Today there was a terrible storm. It took the cowboys an entire day and part of the night to gather all the longhorns that were panic-stricken by the storm. They had escaped in all directions. The result was that 25 longhorns had to be shot, and three horses and one Texan were killed. . . .

The wolves are prowling. We have been here two days skinning and cutting up the slaughtered longhorns.

Disgusted by the sight of our devastated camp, I leave with some emigrants to hunt long-eared hares that the pioneers call jack rabbits, which run everywhere under the horses' hooves. The

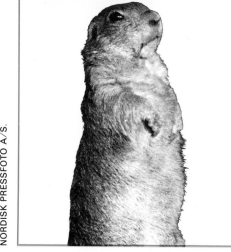

NORDISK PRESSFOTO A/S.

Texans who are with us go after a pack of a hundred deer and kill four of them.

LIBRARY OF CONGRESS

August 12

We have to stop and send some scouts to find a new route, since our trip has become very difficult. The land is riddled with prairie dog holes, and we have had to slaughter another 27 longhorns and six horses that broke their legs in the holes dug by these damned animals. . . . The region is literally swarming with flocks of big birds—sagebrush hens, pintailed grouses, and prairie chickens. These are so easy to hunt that even some of the women and children have joined us. By evening, we have killed several hundred of them . . . but there are also a good number of sprained ankles, and the boss is not happy. Old Jonas' wife

red-spotted wild squirrel with a silvery tail known as the chickaree of the sierra.

Unfortunately, this is not the good season for trapping, but there are so many furry animals that Joe and I will probably give up our mining projects to come back here and lay traps, starting in the month of November. . . .

November 5, 1872

Joe and I started back on the Oregon Trail—1,920 miles on horseback. We crossed the South Pass, where thousands of mustangs are frolicking[3] (which did not prevent a band of Crows from stealing our three best horses).

We have spent the entire autumn here, hunting elk to feed the miners' families. These miners persist in believing that all the streams are filled with gold nuggets. We found something much better. Once the South Pass was crossed, all the forests of the western slope were populated with furry animals, and Joe thinks we can earn a lot more money with their skins than prospecting for gold. . . .

Beaver

was bitten by a rattlesnake, and she probably won't survive. We should have applied a quarter of a warm chicken to the bite, but we didn't have any. . . .

June 1870

Here I am, in Colorado, as a correspondent for the *Rocky Mountain News*. . . . Ever since gold was discovered here in 1859, the white men have flocked to this region. In Denver, I met a former trapper from Ontario, and we left together.

The animals are different from those of the prairie. Buffalo are rare and so are pronghorns, thousands of which you

Wild goats

could still find in Oklahoma. Here there are mostly wild goats, bighorns, and elk. Eagles soar over the mountains.

We take turns with night watch, since grizzlies wander near the camp almost every night. Joe Lafforgue says he would prefer to have to face two Indians empty-handed than one of these bears. They are far more dangerous than the black bears we used to meet in the prairie. . . . We have no problem getting food, since the country is filled with all types of game, especially deer. The deer attract so many mountain lions[2] that we once were able to spot a family of eight hunting together. There are also a lot of porcupines. Joe told me that in Ontario, whites did not hunt these animals, and that they were the only ones you could catch with a club if you were lost in the forest with nothing at all.

We see a great number of small rodents, including woodchucks and pikas, which carry small bundles of hay into crevices in the rocks to eat during the bad season. There is also a kind of

[2] Puma

[3] More than 2,000 wild horses still live in this region. It is the biggest herd in the United States.

Animals in the Indian Economy

OFFICE NATIONAL DU FILM-CANADA

Porcupine
Quills: Used to embroider clothes and children's cradles.

Buffalo
Meat: Mostly eaten fresh during the hunting season; usually roasted on a stick over the fire or boiled, sometimes with vegetables such as wild turnips. The tongue, eyes, kidneys, liver, and brains were considered delicacies. The squaws cut the large pieces of meat into strips, each of which was protected by a layer of fat on one side. These strips were hung to dry in the sun on wooden racks. Once dried, they could be kept for a year without spoiling, and they represented the tribe's food supply. The strips of dried meat were boiled before being eaten. When traveling, warriors carried pemmican, a preparation of dried, powdered buffalo meat to which were added marrow, animal fat, and wild fruits— blueberries, among the Indians of the North.

Fat: The hunters coated their bodies with it to eliminate their own odor when they approached the buffalo on foot.

Skin: Used to make tepees, blankets, clothes, canoes, and travois. The hide was staked down and scraped on both sides, then rubbed with a mixture of liver, fat, and brains. Then it was washed in a stream and softened by pulling it back and forth through a loop of rope. The thickest part of the skin, the part that covered the withers, was used to make shields. Hunters used buffalo skins, and also wolf skins, to disguise their bodies while sneaking up on the

great herds.

Skull: Used to make dishes and bowls.
Brains: Used to soften the skins in the Indian method of tanning.
Bones: The biggest ones were shattered and the marrow was used to prepare pemmican.

The ribs were used to make canoe ribs and curved handles for tomahawks.

The shoulder blades were modified for use as hoes, shovels, and scrapers for tanning the skins.
Horns: Used as powder horns or as boxes in which to store medicinal herbs; they were also used to make arrowheads, knife handles, and trimming for the chief's headdresses.
Teeth: Used in making small tools such as scrapers and paring knives.
Intestines: Used in making rope and bowstrings.
Nerves: Employed as thread for sewing and for bowstrings.
Hooves: Once boiled, they were used in preparing a thick glue.
Bladder: Dried and softened, it was used as a pouch for carrying tobacco or pemmican.
Tail: Used as a flyswatter and as an ornament for the horses.
Manure: Used as a fuel once it was dried in the sun.

Black bear and grizzly bear
Meat: Food, especially among the Sioux, who enjoyed it.
Skin: Clothing for chiefs and witch doctors.
Fat: Mixed with the red sap of a plant called "roucou." The Indians used to smear their bodies with this mixture to protect themselves from mosquito bites.
Claws: Talismans decorating the shaman's, or witch doctor's, clothing. The bear claws were used along with the claws of the lynx and wolf; fox paws; rabbit ears; deer, moose, and buffalo hooves; eagle claws; and owl beaks.

Elk
Skin from the thighs: Used in making high moccasins or leggings without seams; the leg slipped directly into the skin once it was tanned.

Eagle
Feathers: Used for chiefs' headdresses. Those of the Dakota Sioux reached the ground. These feathers were also used in decorating both sacred peace pipes and warriors' spears (along with scalps). Among the Crows, horses also wore a crown of eagle feathers during important ceremonies.

American bald eagle, the emblem of the United States

Whales

During their frequent forays on the Pacific coast, the Blackfoot Indians gathered the long, supple jawbones of the whales washed up on the shores. Without saying where the bones came from, the Blackfeet traded them with the Cheyennes, who used them to make bows. These weapons were highly valued by the warriors because of their mysterious origin and also because their quality was superior to the usual ones, made from ash and reinforced with buffalo tendons.

Shells

These were used, as well as porcupine quills, to make round or oblong beads. The shaping was done by polishing them with fine sand. The round beads were used to decorate clothes and the elongated ones in making arrow-proof vests. The vests were very valuable because of the amount of time spent in making them. When there were no shells, the Sioux used the bones or horns of elk, as well as more and more glass beads that they obtained by trading with peddlers. A handful of these glass beads was worth two or three whalebone bows.

ROGER-VIOLLET

Customs And Legends

OFFICE NATIONAL DU FILM-CANADA

Otter, beaver, ermine, prairie dog, and other small animals

After they were cleaned and tanned, with the skin of the head and paws left intact, these animal hides were made into medicine bags. The Indian usually carried two of them—one contained sacred charms and was carried against his skin; the other contained his pipe, tobacco, war paint, and various pendants. Having his medicine bag snatched by the enemy—or simply losing it—earned the Indian the scorn of his whole tribe. These bags were of various sizes. Some very large ones were made of wolf skin; some smaller ones were made of frog or bird skin.

—When a Havasupai Indian (Arizona) died, he was buried with his boots and saddle at his side. His horse was then sacrificed by driving it off a cliff or by slitting its throat with a knife.

—The Navajo woman who wished to divorce her husband simply took his saddle and placed it outside the door of her hogan (a round wooden hut covered with earth).

—Among the Indians, getting close enough to touch your enemy (called "counting coup" by pioneers) or taking his weapon was a braver deed than killing him.

—For the Sioux, wearing buffalo horns on the head meant having reached the top of the social ladder.

—Even though the Indians had never raised animals for food, one plains tribe, the Mandans, owned turkeys that they kept inside their earthen huts with their wives, children, horses, and dogs.

—An Indian recipe: To cook a rabbit, skin it but leave the head on, then boil it for a long time in a pot. From time to time, lift the cover. When the rabbit's eyes stare at you, it means it is cooked.

*

WIDE WORLD PHOTO

"Long ago, when there were still no birds, the Great Spirit used to grieve each fall when the trees lost their leaves. This is why, one day, he decided to change all the leaves on the trees into birds. The leaves of the red oak became robins, those of the poplar changed into finches, and so on. However, one bird was left out by the Great Spirit, who forgot to give it a color. To hide its despair, this bird soared so high in the sky that it got lost on the way in a field of blue. Some blue clung to its feathers and this is how the bluebird was born."

When the Indians Hunted the Buffalo

The Plains Indians hunted the buffalo in two ways—on foot and on horseback. In either case, those who had guns did not use them, as the pioneers did, because they considered this means of hunting to be unworthy of this marvelous animal, which was so highly regarded in their religion.

Each year, the buffalo made a seasonal migration across the prairie, in a great clockwise circle. In spring they gathered in large herds and headed northwest. The Indians gathered in large groups to hunt them. The buffalo returned across the prairies to the southeast at the end of summer. In late summer, fall, and winter, when grass was scarcer, the buffalo grazed in small herds, and the Indians split up into families or small groups to hunt them.

The spring arrival of the buffalo was eagerly awaited. When the time of their expected coming drew near, the hunters, who were already prepared by a long fast, covered themselves with buffalo skins and danced the Buffalo Dance day and night for several days, acting out all the events of the big hunt they were about to undertake. They believed that this dance always brought the expected result—and sure enough, one morning

their scouts would announce that the buffalo had come.

There were two techniques for approaching the buffalo on foot. In the first one, the Indian smeared his body with animal fat in order to hide his own

odor, and he put on a buffalo skin. Then, patiently, holding a bow, he sneaked into the middle of the unsuspecting herd. He chose the best animals and one by one shot an arrow into the heart of each. The beasts collapsed one after the other, without attracting any attention. However, if the arrow missed its mark and the victim was only wounded, the herd would panic and the hunter would usually be trampled in the ensuing stampede. With the second technique, the Indian, wearing a wolf skin, approached the herd. Upon seeing his hereditary enemy, the closest male buf-

falo charged the intruder, who needed great skill and courage to shoot point blank at this 600-kilogram giant.

Hunting on horseback required the presence of all the men in the tribe. With spears and bows, the galloping hunters encircled the herd so as to set it in motion and make it turn in circles. It was a fantastic spectacle to watch this whirlwind of roaring animals surrounded by galloping riders who were screaming so as to increase the terror of the beasts.

The Indians closed in on the animals and each time one of them got near a buffalo, he shot it with an arrow or dug his spear into its side. The hunt stopped when the chief judged that the number of animals killed was sufficient. The circle of hunters then loosened up and let the buffalo escape. When the dust clouds produced by this terrible battle settled, the dead or wounded buffalo remained on the ground. Often, among them, were bodies of riders thrown from their horses. Frequently, when the circle of riders loosened up to free the herd, an old male turned around to charge the closest Indian. It was an unfortunate hunter who had shot all his arrows and broken his spear.

Covered by wolf skins, hunters approach the herd.

One of the hunters shoots point blank at a charging male.

GLOSSARY

Apache A tribe of warlike nomadic Indians of the southwestern United States

Appaloosa Small sturdy horse bred by the Nez Perce Indians

Arapaho A tribe of nomadic Indians noted for their attacks on wagon trains and settlers

Blackfoot A tribe of nomadic Indians of the plains of the northwestern United States and southern Canada

Cheyenne A tribe of nomadic Indians living in the central plains

Choctaw A tribe of Indians of the south-central United States

Comanche A tribe of Indians of the Shoshone family, living on the western plains

Conestoga wagon A broad-wheeled covered wagon used by pioneers to cross the prairies

Conquistador A Spanish conqueror of America in the 16th century

Corral The circle made by wagon trains at night or when under attack; also, the fenced-in working area on a ranch

Crow A tribe of nomadic plains Indians of the northwestern United States

Frontier The border between a settled area and an unsettled area

Gatling gun An early type of machine gun, which could fire many rounds per minute

Haidas A tribe of Indians of the northern Pacific coast

Home station A station on a stagecoach or Pony Express route where drivers were changed

Hopi A tribe of Pueblo Indians living in adobe towns in the southwestern United States

Immigrant Someone who moves into an area

Kiowas A tribe of nomadic warlike plains Indians

Kwakiutl A tribe of Indians of the northern Pacific coast

Lacrosse A game played with a ball and a long-handled racket, originated by Indians

Locust A type of grasshopper

Longhorn Long-horned cattle once common in the southwestern United States

Mandan A tribe of Indians of the western plains of the United States, famous as traders

Mochila Leather saddlebag used by Pony Express riders

Mustang A small, half-wild, hardy horse of the southwestern United States

Navajo A large tribe of Indians of the southwestern United States

Nez Perce A tribe of Indians of the northwestern United States

Nomadic Traveling from place to place, without a permanent home

Oregon trail The route followed across the western United States by settlers going to the Oregon territory

Pemmican An Indian food; a mixture of dried, powdered buffalo meat, fat, and berries

Pioneer An early settler or colonist

Pony Express The postal system used in the western United States in 1860 and 1861

Prairie schooner A Conestoga wagon, used by pioneers to cross the prairie

Pueblo A group of Indian tribes of the southwestern United States and northern Mexico

Rendezvous A yearly meeting of trappers, merchants, and Indians to exchange goods

Roundup Getting cattle together on the range for sorting or branding

Saloon A place where alcoholic drinks are sold; a bar

Santa Fe trail The trail across the southwestern United States used by wagon trains carrying goods to Santa Fe

Shoshone A group of Indian tribes in the western United States

Sod house A house made of blocks of earth with grass roots, built by pioneers on the plains

Stagecoach A passenger coach that runs between stations; the first regular means of travel across the western United States

Stockade A line of strong posts that form a defensive wall

Swing station A station on a stagecoach or Pony Express route where horses were changed

Thal-Tan A tribe of Indians of upper Canada

Tlingit A group of Indian tribes in northwestern Canada and southeastern Alaska

Travois A wooden framework pulled by a dog or horse, used by the Indians to transport their belongings between campsites

Wagon train A group of wagons used to carry people and goods across the western United States

INDEX

1 2 3 4 5 6 7 8 9 10 —U—85 84 83 82